WALKING ON WATER

AND OTHER BIBLE STORIES

WALKING ON WATER

AND OTHER BIBLE STORIES

ANNE ADENEY

ILLUSTRATED BY RUTH RIVERS

Orion
Children's Books

This edition first published in Great Britain in 2007
by Orion Children's Books
a division of the Orion Publishing Group Ltd
Orion House
5 Upper St Martin's Lane
London WC2H 9EA

1 3 5 7 9 10 8 6 4 2

The stories in this volume were originally published as part of *The Biggest Bible Storybook*,
first published by Orion Children's Books in 2003

Text copyright © Anne Adeney 2003
Illustrations copyright © Ruth Rivers 2003

The rights of Anne Adeney and Ruth Rivers to be identified as the author
and illustrator of this work respectively have been asserted.

Designed by Louise Millar

A catalogue record for this book is available from the British Library.

Printed by Printer Trento, Italy

ISBN 978 1 84255 596 5

Contents

Introduction

I love to hear stories and to tell them too. The Bible is the biggest story-book in the whole world! It is really sixty-six different books all inside one cover, with thousands of stories, but I've picked out fifty of the very best from the New Testament for you.

I'm sure you like to hear stories too. Children have listened to stories since time began and then told them to someone else; maybe their friends, or their brothers and sisters. Then when they grow up, they tell the stories to their own children. This book is full of children telling the stories they have heard or even telling about things they have seen with their own eyes.

The storytellers are all children from long ago, so their way of life was very different from ours. There were no cars in Bible times, or TVs or books like this to read. Children your age even had jobs. They helped look after the animals, usually sheep, goats and donkeys. They helped their parents in their work as fishermen, carpenters, weavers or brickmakers. But even though their way of life was different, they were still children, just like you. They liked to hear stories and to tell them, to laugh, joke and play.

The stories of the New Testament happened thousands of years after the Old Testament stories, around the time Jesus was alive. People lived in towns and cities then, as well as on farms. They would gather in the market-place to meet, shop and talk. The children would go there too, helping their parents or playing with their friends, but always watching and listening to what was going on, so that they could tell stories about everything they saw.

All these stories really happened, a very long time ago. The stories were told over and over again and have been passed down the ages to you. Maybe when you've heard one, you could tell it to someone else, to keep the stories moving through time. The children in this book loved hearing and telling these stories. I hope you do too.

Anne Adeney
Plymouth

JOHN'S STORY

I'm John, son of an incense-maker. We live in Emmaus and my father makes the sweet-smelling stuff that the priests burn in the temple twice a day. Some of the plants you need to make incense grow in our garden and it is my job to cut them and bring them in when my father needs them. He mixes the plants with stuff from fishy-smelling shells to make the incense.

Our family have made incense for many generations and one day I will too. I am even named after another boy called John, whose father's job was to burn incense in the temple. He lived many years before me, in Judea, where I live now.

1
Zechariah meets Gabriel

Zechariah the priest was burning incense on the golden altar while the people prayed outside. Suddenly an angel appeared and Zechariah was very scared.

'Don't be frightened!' said the angel. 'Your wife Elizabeth will have a son called John. He will grow up to be a special man who will prepare the way for the coming of the Lord himself.'

'How can that be true?' asked Zechariah. 'Elizabeth and I are both too old to have children.'

'I'm Gabriel, God's messenger,' said the angel. 'I came to bring you this good news, but because you doubt me, you won't be able to speak until the baby is born.' Then he disappeared.

The people outside wondered why Zechariah was taking so long, but when he came out and couldn't speak, they knew he'd seen a vision. All the time that his wife was pregnant, Zechariah had to use sign language because he remained dumb.

Elizabeth and Zechariah were so happy when the baby was born and their family and friends were delighted. When the baby was eight days old it was time for him to go to the temple for the ceremony of circumcision, which is a special occasion for all Jewish baby boys. Here he would be given his name.

'You'll call him Zechariah, of course, after his father,' their friends said to Elizabeth.

'No, we want to call him John,' said Elizabeth.

'But there's nobody in your family called John!' they said. 'Zechariah, what name do you want?'

Zechariah wrote 'His name is John' on the slate they gave him.

Immediately Zechariah could speak again and praised God for his love and goodness. Everyone in Judea heard about it and wondered what special plans God had for little John.

ANNA'S STORY

My name is Anna and I live in Nain. I have five little sisters and I have to look after them today because my mother is having another baby and my father is busy with his work making mosaic floors. My little sisters never stop chattering!

'Let's call the new baby Phoebe!' said the youngest.

'Or Esther,' said my next sister.

'I want Miriam!' said the next one.

'Abigail's a nice name,' said her twin.

'She should be Ruhammah, after Mother!' said the next.

'It might even be a boy!' I said. 'Then we could call it Amos, after Father.'

Everyone was speechless at the thought of having a boy in the family, so I decided to tell them a story about a very special baby.

2
Gabriel Appears to Mary

God sent his angel Gabriel to Nazareth, where a girl called Mary lived. She was engaged to Joseph, who was descended from King David.

'Greetings to Mary, who has been chosen by God!' said Gabriel.

Mary was frightened at the sight of the angel, who said, 'Don't be afraid. God is pleased with you. You are going to have a baby called Jesus who will rule your people. His kingdom will last for ever.'

'But I'm not even married yet!' said Mary. 'How can I have a baby?'

'The Holy Spirit will make the baby inside you and he will be called the son of God,' said Gabriel. 'Even your cousin Elizabeth is to have a baby in her old age. Nothing is impossible for God!'

'I am God's servant,' said Mary. 'May everything you have said come true.'

The angel disappeared and immediately Mary went to visit her cousin Elizabeth. As soon as they met, the baby inside Elizabeth jumped and kicked. The Holy Spirit filled Elizabeth, so that she knew what Gabriel had said to Mary.

'I'm so happy that the mother of the Lord has come to me!' said Elizabeth. 'When you spoke, the baby inside me jumped for joy! You believed what God told you, so you will really be blessed.'

CALEB'S STORY

I'm Caleb and I'm going to be a carpenter like my father when I grow up. Already I help him by sweeping up the wood shavings and fetching his tools for him. Then I go out to play with the other boys in our town of Magdala. We often talk about what we'll be when we're grown up. Jem says he'll be a fisherman because everyone eats fish. Hiram says he'll be a boat builder because you can't fish without a boat and Sammy says he'll twist the ropes to make the nets. But I'll be a carpenter and make boxes and ploughs and furniture. Jesus, the most important man in the world, was a carpenter. His foster father, Joseph, was a carpenter too and Jesus was born right here in this very town of Bethlehem.

3
The Birth of Jesus

Joseph was a carpenter who lived in Nazareth. Soon his wife Mary was going to have a baby. Then Joseph heard that Augustus, the Roman emperor, had ordered everyone to go to their home towns so he could count them, to work out how much tax money he could collect.

So Joseph and Mary started on the long journey south to Bethlehem.

'I'm tired out, Joseph,' said Mary. 'I hope we can find a place to stay soon.'

But so many people had come to Bethlehem that all the inns were full and they couldn't find a single room to stay in. Eventually they found a stable and decided to rest there for the night because Joseph knew it was nearly time for Mary to have her baby.

There were animals resting in the stable too, but Mary and Joseph were used to that. That night Mary gave birth to a little boy. She wrapped him in strips of cloth to keep him warm and laid him down to sleep on the straw in the animals' manger.

Joseph the carpenter and his wife Mary were overjoyed about the birth of their son, who was also the son of God. They named him Jesus, just as an angel had told them.

TITUS'S STORY

I am Titus, a shepherd boy working in the hills above Hebron. Most of the other shepherds are sleeping, but I'm watching over the flock tonight. Some of the boys hate it. They don't like the dark and are frightened of wolves coming after the sheep. But I like it at nighttime. I've got a big stick strong enough to beat off any wolf and a pile of stones to throw if I hear the slightest noise. But what I like best about the night is the stars. I sit and watch them for hours.

Before we go to sleep the old shepherds always tell stories. My favourite story is about shepherds just like us, who got to meet the King of Heaven.

4
What the Shepherds Saw

Near Bethlehem there were shepherds keeping watch over their flock by night. Suddenly an angel appeared to them and dazzled them with the glory of God. The shepherds were all very frightened, but the angel said, 'Don't be afraid! I've come with a message of great joy for you and everyone else. Tonight a baby has been born in Bethlehem and he is to be your Saviour, Christ the Lord. You will find him wrapped in strips of cloth and lying on a bed of straw in a manger.'

As soon as the angel finished speaking,
the whole sky was filled with angels, singing praises to God.

'Glory to God and peace to all his people on earth!' they sang.

The shepherds couldn't take their eyes off the angels, but as soon as
they'd gone they said, 'Let's go to Bethlehem! God has told us about this
special baby, so now we must go and see him for ourselves!'

They hurried into the town and found Mary and Joseph in the stable,
and the baby lying in the manger, just as the angel had told them. They knelt
and worshipped the baby who was the son of God. Then they went and told
everyone else about what had happened, praising God for everything they
had seen and heard.

CILLA'S STORY

My name is Cilla and my father makes the dyes to colour the yarn the women use to weave into clothes. He made the blue and crimson dyes that my friend Shua's mother used to make her fine new robe. He uses plants and crushed insects to make the dyes, which makes our home a very smelly place! Shua's new robe was so gorgeous that I wondered if it was even more beautiful than the robes of the Magi, the wise men who came when Jesus was born.

5
The Coming of the Wise Men

After Jesus was born, three wise men came to Jerusalem. 'Where is he who is born King of the Jews?' they asked everyone they met. 'We have followed a star from the East and have come to worship him.'

King Herod ruled the Israelites at the time and he was very worried when he heard about this new king. He didn't want anyone coming to take over from him. So Herod got the wise men to visit him secretly.

'Where is this new king,' he asked them, 'and when did this star appear?'

When he heard that Jesus had been born in Bethlehem, he told the wise men to go and worship him.

'Be sure you return and tell me where the baby king is', he said. 'I want to worship him too!'

But he planned to kill Jesus and thought he could trick the wise men into telling him where Jesus was. So the Magi headed towards Bethlehem, following the star. They were filled with joy when the star shone over the stable and they knew they had found the new king at last.

When they went inside and found Mary holding baby Jesus, they fell to their knees and worshipped him. Then they got out the fine gifts they had brought all the way from the East and gave him presents of gold, frankincense and myrrh.

That night they had a dream that warned them not to go back to King Herod, so they went home a different way.

JUDE'S STORY

My name is Jude and I'm travelling with my father to sell the pomegranates he grows on our smallholding. Every week we ride into town on our donkeys. Riding the donkey is much better than walking because I can see so much more. I can see geckos sunning themselves on the rocks. It's great up here! My donkey rides are fun, but I remember the story of Mary and Joseph escaping from King Herod's men. That must have been really scary.

6
Escape from Herod

After the wise men had left the stable, Mary settled Jesus in the manger again and they all went to sleep. Joseph dreamed that an angel came to him and said, 'Get up quickly, Joseph! Take Mary and the child and escape to Egypt. You are in great danger here because Herod is looking for Jesus so he can kill him! Stay in Egypt until I tell you that it's safe to come home.'

So Joseph woke Mary and put her and the sleeping baby on to his donkey. He packed the precious gifts that the wise men had given Jesus and some food for the journey and they left Bethlehem straight away.

King Herod was furious when he found out that the wise men had tricked him and gone home without telling him where to find Jesus. So he called his soldiers and ordered them to kill every baby boy in Bethlehem who was less than two years old. The soldiers did what he ordered and slaughtered all the baby boys. Only Jesus escaped because he was safely in Egypt.

Soon after, wicked King Herod died. The angel came back to Joseph in a dream and said, 'It's safe to take your family back to Israel now because the one who was trying to kill Jesus is dead.'

So they all went back to Israel. But when they got there they found that Herod's son was now king and they were frightened of him too. So Joseph loaded up his donkey again and took his family to the province of Galilee, where they settled in the town of Nazareth.

STEPHEN'S STORY

I am Stephen and I sell doves near the temple in Jerusalem. Not long ago a girl asked to buy my two very best birds because her brother was being dedicated at the temple. This is our custom of families taking new babies to the temple to say thank you to God for them, by making a sacrifice of birds or a lamb. My mother told me this story of Mary and Joseph bringing Jesus to be dedicated.

7

Dedication of Jesus

When Jesus was old enough, Mary and Joseph brought him to Jerusalem to be dedicated to God in the temple. They offered two young birds as a sacrifice for the gift of a fine son. There was a very holy man in Jerusalem, called Simeon. He was very old, but God had promised him that he would not die before he saw Jesus, the promised saviour.

The Holy Spirit told Simeon to go to the temple on the day of Jesus's dedication. When Simeon saw Jesus, he knew he was the saviour. He was very excited and asked to hold the baby.

'Now I can die in peace and happiness because God has kept his promise to me,' said Simeon. 'For this is the baby he sent to save the world!'

Mary and Joseph were astonished as they listened to him. Then Simeon said to Mary, 'Your son will bring great joy to you and to many others, but he will give you great sadness too and make many people in this land very angry.'

Then an old lady called Anna came up to them. She was a holy woman and spent all her time in the temple, praying to God. She was thrilled to see baby Jesus and gave great thanks to God. She already knew that Jesus had come to save the people of Israel when he grew up.

When the dedication was finished, Mary and Joseph took Jesus back to their home in Nazareth, where he grew to be strong. Even as a little boy, Jesus was so wise he could understand God's teachings better than some grown-ups.

MICHAEL'S STORY

I'm Michael, a rabbi's son. It's hard being a teacher's son! Everyone expects me to be very clever and I'm not. We speak Aramaic at home, like everyone else, but at school I have to learn Hebrew, so I can read our holy book, the Torah. But I'm not very good at it at all! My sisters are lucky because girls don't go to school. They stay at home and learn to weave and cook and keep house. My father says I have to learn lots of the Torah by heart before I am even as old as Jesus was, when his parents lost him in Jerusalem.

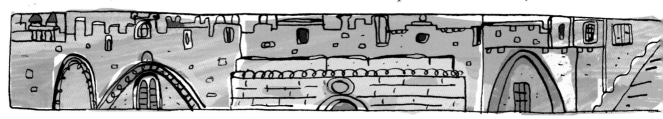

8
Jesus in His Father's House

Every year Joseph and Mary took Jesus up to Jerusalem to celebrate the feast of Passover. The year Jesus was twelve was one Mary would always remember. When the feast was over, they set off back to Nazareth. They travelled with all their friends and relations, so there were hundreds of donkeys and carts and many people walking alongside. It was a noisy, bustling group, as everyone talked about what they had seen in the city and the wonders of the huge temple.

Joseph travelled with the men and thought that Jesus was with his mother. Mary was with the women and young children and thought that now Jesus was twelve, he must be travelling with the men. So neither of them missed Jesus for a whole day.

When they discovered he was missing they were very worried.

'Have you seen Jesus?' they asked everyone.

'We haven't seen Jesus since we left Jerusalem!' they all replied.

Frantic with worry, they headed back to the city. For three long, frightening days they searched for Jesus. Then they went to the temple to pray and there they found him. Jesus was sitting with all the teachers of the Law, listening to them and asking the most difficult questions. Everyone who heard him was amazed at the young boy's understanding and his answers.

But his mother wasn't impressed.

'Where do you think you've been?' she demanded. 'We've been looking for you everywhere! We were beside ourselves with worry!'

'Why did you search for me?' Jesus asked. 'Didn't you realise that I would be in my Father's house?'

At the time they didn't understand what Jesus meant, they were just relieved to have found him. They went back home to Nazareth and Jesus became even cleverer as he grew older. Jesus was always obedient to his parents after that and everyone who knew him loved him.

NATHAN'S STORY

My name is Nathan and I sell sandals. My father makes the best sandals in the whole city! I help my mother sell them in the market at Jotapata. There are lots of people selling things – fruits, cloth, cheese, jewellery – so it's important to attract people to our stall. We don't want them wasting their money on pomegranates when they could be buying a pair of Father's sandals! He even made sandals for Jesus, the famous preacher. I heard the story of when Jesus was baptised.

9

John Baptises Jesus

John the Baptist, son of Elizabeth and Zechariah, lived in the wilderness. He wore a tunic made of camel's hair and ate locusts and wild honey. Crowds of people came out into the desert to hear him preach.

'If you tell God that you are sorry for the bad things you have done, he will forgive you!' he told them. To prepare them for the coming of Jesus, John baptised people in the river Jordan. It was a way of showing that they had turned away from their old lives and wanted to start over again. Some of the religious leaders pretended to be good, but John knew that they would never really change their ways.

'Stop pretending to be good, you snakes!' he ordered them. 'Soon someone else will be coming to teach you', he told the crowds. 'He's much more important than me! I'm not even good enough to untie his sandals for him, like a servant. And while I baptise you with water, he will baptise you with the Holy Spirit.'

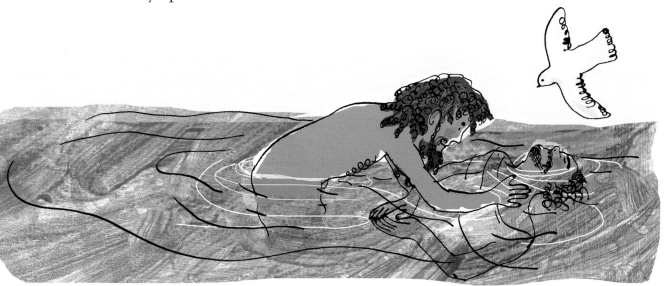

The man John was talking about was Jesus. One day Jesus joined the crowd and asked John to baptise him. John knew that Jesus was so important that it should have been the other way round. Jesus should have been baptising him.

'It's what God wants for me', Jesus told his cousin gently.

So John dipped Jesus down into the river to baptise him. As he stood up, the Holy Spirit appeared over his head in the shape of a dove and everyone heard a voice from heaven say, 'This is my own dear son, in whom I am well pleased.'

JEMIMAH'S STORY

My name is Jemimah and I have to help my mother make lots of bread for the shepherds every day.

'Tending the flocks makes them hungry!' my mother says, stirring water into the flour for another batch of bread. 'It's a pity we couldn't make lots before they came home, but you know how hard and stale this sort of bread gets if you don't eat it at once.'

'It would be so much easier if we could just tell the stones to turn into bread, like the devil told Jesus to do, in the desert!' I sighed, as I flipped over yet another thin circle of bread.

10
Bread from Stones?

After John had baptised Jesus, the Holy Spirit took him out into the desert so that the devil could test him. Jesus ate nothing, so after forty days and forty nights he was very hungry.

The devil tried to tempt him. 'If you're God's son', he said, 'why don't you use your powers to turn these stones into loaves of bread?'

But Jesus said, 'No! The Scriptures tell us that we need more than bread to live on. We need to obey every word that God has spoken.'

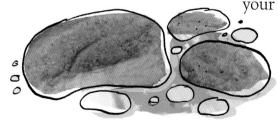

Then the devil took him to the high top of the Temple in Jerusalem and tried to test him again.

'Why don't you jump off here, Jesus, and prove you are the Son of God?' he said. 'The Scriptures promise that God will send his angels to catch you.'

'No!' said Jesus. 'God says we should not play foolish games to test him!'

So the devil took Jesus to a high mountain where he could see the whole world. 'I will give you power over all this if you will worship me as your master instead of God,' he said.

'Get out of here, Satan!' said Jesus. 'The only person I will ever worship is the Lord God!'

The devil knew that Jesus was too strong to be tempted, so he left him alone. Then God sent his angels to look after Jesus and care for him.

JETHRO'S STORY

I am Jethro and my family are all fishermen on the Sea of Galilee.

'Can I go fishing with you this evening?' I asked, as my brother and I helped our uncles wash out their nets. 'I can catch a thousand tilapia in one net!'

'My net will break if there's a thousand tilapia in it,' said my uncle, 'so you'd better learn how to mend it first, just in case!'

'Maybe we'll catch as many as Jesus did, when he went out in Simon Peter's boat,' I said. 'There were so many that the boat nearly sank from the weight!'

11
Fishers of Men

Jesus was teaching the word of God on the shores of Galilee. There were so many people eager to hear him that he was nearly trampled by the crowds. His friend Simon Peter was a fisherman, so Jesus got into his boat and asked him to push it out a little way into the water. Then he was able to speak to the people without being crushed.

When he'd finished speaking Jesus said to Simon Peter, 'Go out into the deep part of the lake and cast your nets!'

'We've been out all night and we didn't catch a thing!' said Simon Peter. 'But if you insist, we'll have another go.'

So they sailed out into the lake. To Simon Peter's amazement, the nets were soon so full of fish that they were starting to rip!

'James! John! Get over here quickly!' he yelled across the water. 'I've got a huge catch!'

His partners immediately came to help and took lots of the fish into their boat. Soon the two boats were so full of fish that they were in danger of sinking. Simon Peter and the others realised that they were seeing a miracle happen in front of their eyes.

'Don't come near me, Lord!' said Simon Peter, falling to his knees. 'I'm a sinful person and don't deserve to be near you!'

'Don't worry!' said Jesus kindly. 'From now on you'll all be coming with me and fishing for men!'

So, after that day, Simon Peter, James and John left their nets and followed Jesus.

BETH'S STORY

I am Beth and I'm very excited because my uncle is getting married today. I've been helping my mother and grandmother cook for ages because the feasting will go on for days. They've already had the betrothal ceremony and exchanged gifts.

Now my uncle has gone to the bride's house to get her and be blessed. Then he'll lead her back through the village to our house. My brothers and sisters and all the guests are all lined up along the path to welcome them. I think it must be just like the wedding Jesus went to in Cana.

12
Water into Wine

Mary was invited to a marriage feast in Cana. Her son Jesus and his disciples were guests at the wedding too. After much feasting, the wine ran out. Mary told Jesus what had happened.

'There's no wine left,' she said. 'It's all been drunk, but the party is still going on!'

'Why are you telling me?' asked Jesus. 'It's not my problem. Nor is it time for me to do miracles.'

But still his mother called the servants over and said, 'Do whatever my son tells you.'

They went to Jesus and asked him what they should do about the wine. Jesus pointed to six big water jars standing in the corner.

'Fill them up with water,' he said.

The jars were huge, holding about thirty gallons of water each, but the servants filled them up with buckets of fresh water. When this was done they came back for more instructions.

'Pour some out and ask the master of the feast to try it,' said Jesus.

When the man tasted the water he was amazed.

'This is wonderful wine!' he told the bridegroom. 'Usually people serve the best wine first. Guests won't notice if it's not so good later on because they've already drunk so much! But you've saved the very best wine until last!'

This was the very first time that Jesus performed a miracle, by changing the water into wine to please his mother. It also showed his powers to his disciples, who put their trust in him.

DAN'S STORY

My name is Dan and my father is a tassel maker. All the men wear prayer shawls when they go to the synagogue and each shawl has four special tassels. But the poor lepers don't have prayer shawls, just torn rags to cover their thin, misshapen bodies. Leprosy is a really nasty disease and it's catching. That's why they live apart from everyone.

Although the leper colony is outside our town, I often see them in the distance, shouting, 'Unclean, unclean!' to make sure nobody goes near them. They are always dirty and very thin because they have so little to eat. They are not allowed to work, so they have to beg for food. They look so ill and miserable that I feel sorry for them. My mother often gives me bread to take to the lepers. I leave the bread at the bottom of the hill and they come down and get it, just as the lepers must have done in the time of Jesus.

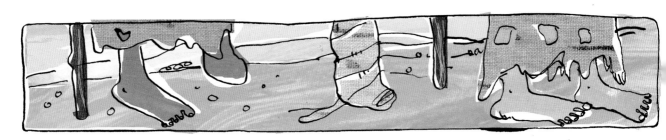

13
The Grateful Leper

While he was on his way to Jerusalem, Jesus saw ten lepers in the distance. They recognised Jesus and had heard of his miracles, so they cried out to him, saying, 'Have pity on us, Jesus!'

He went right up to them and said, 'Go and show yourselves to the priests, so they may know that you are cured of your disease and give you permission to mix with people again.'

While they were on their way to the priests, all ten were cured of their disease. One of these men was a Samaritan, a man from another country. As soon as he realised that his sore body had been made whole, he began to praise God. He ran back to Jesus and threw himself into the dust at his feet.

'Thank you, Jesus!' he cried.

'Didn't I heal ten of you?' asked Jesus. 'Yet only a foreigner was grateful enough to come back and thank God. Get up and go on your way. You are completely healed because you trusted in me.'

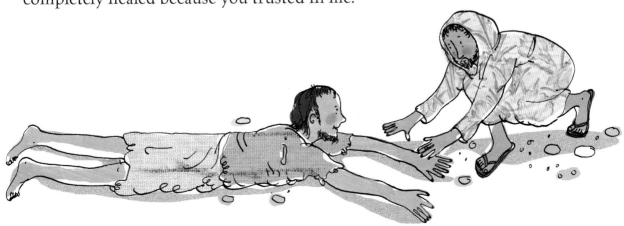

RUFUS'S STORY

I am Rufus, the son of a soldier. My father is a centurion, which means he is in charge of a hundred men in the Roman army and everyone respects him here in Capernaum. Yesterday, our servant Cornelius became ill. He couldn't move and everyone said he was going to die. We were all very sad, because we love Cornelius. He's been in our family since before I was born. But today he's just as well as can be! It's all because Jesus healed him with a miracle.

14
The Centurion's Servant

One day a centurion asked the elders of the Jews to help his slave, who was very dear to him, but about to die from a painful disease. They went to Jesus and said to him, 'Please help this Roman centurion, because he deserves it. He has been good to all the Jews and has even built us a new synagogue to worship in!'

Jesus met the centurion and said to him, 'I will happily come to your house and heal your servant.'

But the centurion said, 'No, please don't take the trouble to do that. I am not worthy to have a man such as you at my house. But I know you are so powerful you don't even have to see my servant to help him. I'm a powerful man too, so I know about such things. I tell my soldiers and my servants to come here and go there and they do it right away! All you have to do is say the word, and I believe my servant will be healed!'

Jesus was amazed that the man trusted in him so much. He turned to the crowd and said, 'I have never met a man with as much faith as this centurion, not even in Jerusalem!'

He turned to the Roman soldier and said, 'Go on home now and you will find that your dear servant is cured.'

When the centurion got home he found that his servant was already out of bed and completely well. He had been healed at the exact moment that Jesus had spoken.

JOANNA'S STORY

My name's Joanna and I am a rope maker's daughter. I have a sister called Helah and lots of brothers. We all live in the town of Caesarea. Helah and I help our mother in the house. It's our job to fold up the family's sleeping mats and then to grind the corn for the bread mother will bake later. We usually do most of our chores up on the flat roof because it's much cooler there, but at the moment there's a hole in the roof. I will be glad when Father mends the hole, which has been getting bigger all week.

Sometimes people make holes in the roof on purpose! I know a story about a man who was paralysed. His friends couldn't get him near enough to hear Jesus, so they let him down through the roof!

15
Through the Roof!

Large crowds followed Jesus everywhere. They wanted to hear his stories about God's forgiveness and to see him perform miracles, like healing the sick. One day he was talking to the people in a house in Capernaum. So many had squeezed in to hear him that there was no space left anywhere.

Then four men arrived, carrying their friend on a mat because he couldn't walk. They wanted to ask Jesus to make him better, but they could not get into the house to ask him because of all the other people. So they climbed the outside stairs to the flat roof and cut a big hole in it. Then they lowered their friend down on his mat, into the room where Jesus was speaking.

Jesus saw that the men all had faith in him, so he said to the sick man, 'My friend, your sins are forgiven.'

There were some religious leaders there, listening to Jesus. They were shocked to hear him say this because they knew that only God could forgive sins. Although they said nothing Jesus knew what they were thinking.

'Why do you question what I say?' he asked them. 'Which is easier, to forgive this man's sins or to make him walk again? To prove that I have the right to forgive his sins, I will also heal him.'

He said to the paralysed man, 'Get up, pick up your mat and take it home with you!'

The man immediately got up, folded the mat he had lain on for so long, and walked out. The crowd were astounded at this incredible miracle. 'We've never seen anything like this before!' they said and went away praising God.

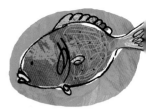

ZEB'S STORY

My name is Zeb and I live in Joppa, where I'm learning to be a fisherman. Ezra is teaching me to cast a net. I twirled round, flung out my arms and let go. Instead of the circular net coming back down on top of me, its hard little weights bouncing painfully all over my body as usual, it spun round in a graceful arc and landed flat on the water. Ezra helped me haul in the rope at the centre of the net, which had caught several fish underneath it.

'Your first catch, Zeb!' said Ezra. 'You must be the smallest fisherman who ever learnt to cast such a big net!'

'Thank you for teaching me, Ezra!' I said. 'I've got nothing to give you in return – except a fish and you've got lots of those!'

'Tell me one of your mother's stories then, lad,' said Ezra.

16
Jesus Calms the Storm

Jesus had spent a busy day teaching the crowds by the lakeside and now he was exhausted. 'Let's go over to the other side of the lake,' he said to his disciples. So they all got into one of the fishing boats and sailed off across the calm lake. Putting a cushion under his head, Jesus was soon fast asleep in the stern of the boat.

Suddenly a strong wind blew across the lake. Great walls of water crashed against the sides of the boat, making it toss about violently. Huge waves flooded over the boat and began to fill it up. But Jesus was very tired and slept on. The disciples were used to bad weather, as most of them were fishermen, but this storm was worse than anything they'd ever seen and they were terrified.

'Wake up, Jesus!' they yelled at him. 'Look at this terrible storm! The boat's sinking and we're all going to drown! Don't you even care?'

But Jesus wasn't afraid. He stood up and quietly spoke to the wind and the waves. 'Be still!' he said. Straight away the wind died down, the waves stopped and all was calm and peaceful once more.

'Why were you scared?' Jesus asked his friends. 'After all that you've seen me do, why didn't you trust me to take care of you?'

The disciples were amazed and said to each other, 'Who can this man be, that even the wind and the raging seas obey him?'

PRISCILLA'S STORY

My name is Priscilla and my father breeds horses. The most amazing thing has just happened to my best friend! I ran home quickly to tell everyone.

'Father, Father! You'll never guess what happened to Elizabeth!' I yelled, before I was even through the front door. 'It was terrible, Father! Elizabeth died this morning!'

'Elizabeth's dead, Priscilla! How sad!' said Father.

'No Father, she's not dead! She was dead and we were all crying and wailing. Then Jairus got Jesus, and he brought her back to life again! I was right outside the door when it happened and afterwards I spread honey on some bread for her and she ate it!'

'Tell me exactly what happened,' said Father.

17
'Get up, Little Girl!'

Jesus was teaching a large crowd of people beside the Sea of Galilee when Jairus, a synagogue leader, came up to him. He fell on his knees and begged Jesus, 'My little girl is dying! Won't you please come and help her?'

So Jesus went with him. On the way there he healed a woman who had been sick for twelve years. While he was talking to her, some messengers arrived from Jairus's house.

'There's no point in bothering Jesus any more,' they said sadly. 'Your daughter is already dead!'

But Jesus just said, 'Don't worry, Jairus, believe in me!'

He told everyone to wait where they were and just took his friends Peter, James and John with him. Before they got to the house they could hear the sound of dozens of people weeping and wailing at the tops of their voices.

'What's all the noise about?' asked Jesus. 'Your child is not dead, she's just asleep.'

Everyone laughed at him then because they knew for sure that she had died. So he sent them all out of the house and went in with his friends and the girl's parents. He took her hand and said quietly, 'Get up, little girl!'

Instantly the child opened her eyes and got up. Everyone gasped, then all began to talk at once, amazed by this miracle.

'The child must be hungry,' said Jesus. 'Somebody should get her some food.' Then he warned them not to tell anyone what had happened.

ZEKE'S STORY

My name's Zeke and my father is a trader who travels a lot. Sometimes he brings home some strange things. Today he gave me some foreign coins he had collected on his travels. They were nothing like the Jewish coins we were used to.

'Are you sure it's real money, Zeke?' asked my sister Riz. 'It doesn't even have a palm tree on it!'

'It's real enough, just foreign,' I said. 'You'll be able to buy that new bracelet you want and I'll be able to buy a lamb of my own at last! But first we must take it to Tiras, the money-changer, and hope he doesn't cheat us, as usual!'

'Let's go up to the Temple then,' said Riz. 'I want to buy my new bracelet today.'

'The money-changers aren't in the Temple courtyard any more,' I replied. 'Didn't you hear what happened yesterday? Jesus called them all robbers and drove them out! I was up there to buy some birds to sacrifice when Father came home and I saw it all!'

18
Den of Thieves

When Jesus came up to Jerusalem he went to the Temple. In the outer courtyards people were selling and trading cows, sheep and doves. The cheating money-changers were haggling over piles of foreign coins, trying to trade them for as little Jewish money as possible.

Jesus was horrified. This was his Father's house where people came to pray and worship and the merchants had made it like a noisy, smelly market-place.

He took some rope, knotted it into a whip and made them all leave the Temple. He drove out the animals and turned over the tables of the money-changers.

'Get these beasts out of here!' he shouted. 'This is meant to be a house of prayer! What right have you to turn it into a den of thieves?'

His followers had never seen him so angry, but they remembered the verse in Scripture that foretold that he would defend the house of God.

Many of the chief priests of the Temple were greedy and wicked. They took advantage of the people and cheated them. So when they heard what Jesus had done they looked for a way to destroy him. They were worried that the people might rebel and join Jesus and that there would be riots in the city and they would lose their power.

ETHAN'S STORY

My name is Ethan. My father is a barley farmer in Judea and one day I will be one too. I watch my father and listen to everything he tells me.

'You must plant seeds in good rich soil,' he says. 'Make sure they get water and sunshine and don't get choked by weeds. Then they will grow tall and strong.'

Then he told me a story about seeds – one Jesus used to tell.

19
The Sower and the Seeds

A farmer went to sow some seeds on his land. He threw big handfuls of the seed all around him. Some of it fell on the hard path where he was standing. As soon as the farmer walked away, hungry birds swooped down and ate it all up.

Some seed fell on rocky patches of ground, where there was just a thin layer of soil. The seeds grew up quickly at first. The roots reached down into the soil for moisture but because of the rock underneath they could not grow far. They could not soak up enough water and so the hot sun shrivelled them up and they died.

Some seeds landed on ground that was full of thorns and thistles and other weeds. The weeds grew strongly and took all the food and water from the seeds. Some of the little plants were overcome by the weeds and died.

40

Some seeds fell upon very rich soil and grew to be big strong plants, a hundred times as large as the farmer had planted.

Then Jesus said to his audience, 'If anyone has listening ears, now's the time to use them and try to understand what I mean by this story!'

But his followers were puzzled. 'What does this story mean?' they asked him.

Jesus replied, 'The seeds are like the message I am trying to tell you about the kingdom of God. The seed that fell on the hard path is like the person who hears my message but doesn't understand

it. The devil comes and takes away what has been sown in that person's heart, just as the birds took away the seeds.

'The seed that fell on rocky ground is like the person who hears my message gladly and is happy to hear the news. But without roots, nothing can survive. As soon as something bad happens to that person, they forget my message.

'The seed that fell amongst the thorns and weeds is like a person who hears my message but has so many other cares and worries that he does not have time or space to concentrate on it. Everything he has heard is lost.

'The seed that falls on rich soil is like the person who hears my words, understands them completely and keeps on believing in me. That person can then go out and convince a hundred or more people that the word of God is true. This is what the story of the sower and the seeds is all about.'

NAOMI'S STORY

My name is Naomi and my family has a bread stall in the market-place.

'You're good at selling, Naomi; that's the last loaf gone!' said my mother today.

'I heard a wonderful story about Jesus just now,' I said, brushing the last specks of flour from my hands.

'Jesus the teacher?' said Mother. 'His followers have bought loaves of bread for him here before now.'

'Yes, but he doesn't seem to need very many,' I said. 'I heard that when he was on the hillside at Tabgha the other day he fed more than five thousand people with only two small fishes and a few loaves of bread!'

20
Five Loaves and Two Fishes

The disciples had come back from teaching the people and were eager to tell Jesus what they had done. But there were so many people around that there was no chance to talk or rest. Jesus was also very sad because he had just heard that King Herod had killed his cousin John.

'Let's go somewhere far away across the lake,' he said. 'We can be alone there and you can rest from your travels.'

But some people heard where they were heading and spread the word. Many raced ahead on foot, so that by the time Jesus and his disciples got there the hillside was covered with people. When Jesus saw them he was filled with pity.

'They're milling around like sheep without a shepherd,' he said. 'I must teach them.' He taught them all day and then everyone started to feel hungry.

'You'd better send them into the nearest town to buy themselves some food,' said the disciples.

'They don't need to do that,' said Jesus. 'Why don't you feed them?'

'We can't afford to feed all these people!' they said crossly. 'There must be thousands of them!'

'A little boy over there has five small loaves of bread and two fishes,' said Andrew. 'But that won't feed very many.'

'Get everyone to sit down on the grass,' said Jesus, 'and bring the food to me.'

Jesus prayed and broke the five small loaves into pieces. Then he gave them to the disciples to share out between the people. Next he did the same thing with the fishes. As they gave out the food they found that there was more than enough for everyone! Everyone picnicking on the grass had as much as they wanted to eat and when they gathered up the bread and fish that was left over, there were twelve whole baskets full.

BARNEY'S STORY

I'm Barney and I've just come to live in Tiberias with my Uncle Lud, who is a fisherman. He promised to take me out in his boat on a calm day. But now the day has come I'm very scared because I used to live in the hills and I've never been in a boat before.

'Don't worry, I'll teach you to be a fisherman yet!' said Uncle Lud. 'Just look at that water. It's as still as the floor in our house! It looks as if you could almost walk across it to catch your fish!'

'Jesus could walk on water!' I said.

'That sounds like a good story!' said Uncle Lud.

So I told him the story to take my mind off the rocking boat.

21
Walking on Water

Jesus had been teaching crowds of people all day. He'd even had to feed all five thousand of them because they'd refused to go home and followed him wherever he went. Now it was getting late.

'I'll talk to these people again, then send them on their way,' said Jesus, after he had fed them all by a miracle. 'You get into your boat and sail back to the other side of the lake,' he told the disciples.

After everyone had gone, Jesus climbed up the mountainside to pray by himself. Night fell and out on the lake the disciples were in trouble. Strong winds had blown up, as they often did on the Sea of Galilee, and huge waves were pounding the sides of the boat and soaking the tired men.

At about four o'clock in the morning the disciples saw a figure walking towards them across the raging waters. 'It's a ghost!' they screamed in terror.

'Don't be afraid!' said Jesus. 'It's me!'

'If it's really you, Lord, tell me to walk out to you on the water!' said Peter.

'All right', said Jesus. 'Come out here to me.'

So Peter climbed over the side of the boat and started off. At first he looked straight at Jesus and walked on the water towards him with no trouble. But then he began to feel the force of the wind and saw the big waves crashing around him. He was overcome by fear and at that moment he began to sink.

'Save me, Lord!' he screamed.

Instantly Jesus reached out his hand and rescued him.

'Why didn't you trust me, Peter?' he asked. 'Where is your faith?'

They walked back to the boat together and as soon as they climbed aboard, the winds calmed down and the big waves disappeared. The rest of the disciples fell down on their knees and worshipped Jesus.

'You really are the son of God!' they cried.

BARNEY'S STORY

I loved my fishing trip with my uncle! No storms blew up as we fished and I didn't even feel seasick. Uncle Lud taught me how to heave in the long net and then to sort all the different sorts of fish we caught.

'These little ones are lake sardines,' he said, 'but these big tilapia are much the best! Look at this one, Barney. They seem to be attracted to shiny things too. Do you know why people call them St Peter's fish?'

'Yes, my mother told me the story!' I exclaimed. 'It was when Jesus and Peter needed money to pay to the government for their taxes. But they didn't have any because they spent all their time teaching the people.'

22

Fishing for Taxes

When Jesus and the disciples were in Capernaum, a tax collector came to Peter and said, 'Do you and your master intend to pay your taxes? You owe half a shekel each.'

'Don't worry, we'll pay up soon,' said Peter. 'I'll just go and ask my master about it.'

He went to Jesus, but before he could even ask him, Jesus said, 'Who do you think the king should take money from, Peter? From his sons or from foreign visitors?'

'From the foreigners!' said Peter.

'Then the sons will be free,' said Jesus. 'But we should not offend the tax collectors, so we'd better pay up.'

'But we have no money, Lord, and we owe half a shekel each!' said Peter. 'What shall we do?'

'Go down to the shore, Peter, and take with you a line and hook,' said Jesus. 'Cast your line into the water and start fishing. Take the very first fish that you catch and look into its mouth.'

Peter did exactly what Jesus told him. He cast his line into the lake and very quickly caught a big tilapia. He pulled it ashore and opened its mouth. There inside was a one shekel coin, exactly enough to pay the taxes for Jesus and himself.

KEREN'S STORY

My name is Keren and my mother is a washerwoman. I live with my parents and sisters beside the River Jordan. Every day my sisters and I help our mother wash clothes on the riverbank.

'Keren and Martha, you take the ends of the basket and, Adah, you carry the smaller bundle,' said Mother, as she squeezed the water out of a cloth and laid it on top of the big basket.

I quite like washing clothes on the riverbank, although Mother has to do all the wringing out, as you need really strong hands for that. The worst bit about washing is hauling it all back to the house to be hung out to dry. Clothes are so much heavier when they are wet.

'You girls take that lot back and put it to dry, while I wash the rest,' Mother said.

We carried the washing back and started spreading it out on our flat roof, where the hot sun would soon dry it.

'Mother is the best washerwoman in the whole town!' I said as we laid the clean washing out. 'These clothes look nearly as bright as the ones Jesus wore when he was glorified by God!'

23
My Beloved Son

Jesus took Peter, James and John up on to a high mountain. Suddenly Jesus was changed right in front of their eyes. His ordinary, dusty robe was turned into one of dazzling white and his face shone like the brightest sun. To the amazement of the disciples, Moses and Elijah appeared. These famous men had been dead for thousands of years, but now they were there on the mountainside, talking with Jesus!

'This is wonderful!' said Peter. 'Shall I make a shelter for each of you here?'

But just then a bright cloud came down and covered all of them. From inside the cloud came the voice of God, saying, 'This is my beloved son. Listen to everything he says because I am very pleased with him!'

The disciples were so frightened to hear God speaking that they threw themselves face down on the ground and covered their heads with their hands. They lay there, terrified, until they felt Jesus touch each of them gently.

'Don't be afraid,' he said. 'You can get up now.'

When Peter, James and John got up and looked around them, they saw that there was nobody there but Jesus. As they walked back down the mountain, Jesus said to them, 'Don't say anything about what you have seen here today until I have risen from the dead.'

JOSH'S STORY

I am Josh. My father has an inn on the road from Jerusalem to Jericho. It is a long, steep road and there are often robbers lurking in the rocks on each side of the road. I am quite safe here at the inn, but I get to know a lot of the travellers who come here and I worry about them as they set off on their journeys.

It is safer for them to travel in groups, but that is not always possible. But even as I worry, I am comforted by the thought of a story Jesus told, about how a foreigner helped a traveller who was robbed on the road. This is the story that Jesus told.

24
The Kind Samaritan

Once a teacher of the Law asked Jesus, 'What do I have to do to live for ever in heaven?'

'What does the Scripture tell you to do?' asked Jesus.

'It says I should love God with all my heart, soul, mind and strength and it also tells me to love my neighbour as much as I love myself', said the teacher. 'But who is my neighbour? Is it just the man who lives next door or also people from the same town or the same country? Could foreigners be my neighbours too?'

'Listen to this story', said Jesus. 'Then tell me who is your neighbour. A Jew was travelling on the long road from Jerusalem to Jericho. He was attacked by thieves, who beat him up, took everything he had, and left him to die in the hot sun.'

'Later, a Jewish priest came along and saw him. But, instead of helping the poor man, he walked by on the other side of the road and pretended he hadn't seen him.

'Then a Jewish man, who worked in the Temple, came along. He too passed by on the other side of the road, ignoring the man's cries for help.

'Eventually a Samaritan arrived. He was a man of a foreign race, who were all looked down on and hated by the Jews. Although he realised that the man who had been robbed was a Jew, he immediately ran to help him. He tended the man's injuries, then helped him on to his own donkey. He led the donkey to an inn, where he paid the innkeeper to look after the poor man until he was better.'

When Jesus had finished this story, he asked the teacher, 'Which of the men acted like a neighbour to the man who was attacked and robbed?'

'It was the Samaritan who showed kindness to him,' said the teacher.

'Then you must go and do the same,' said Jesus.

SUSANNAH'S STORY

My name is Susannah. The carob trees that my family grow surround our house. My father and brothers tend them and pick the pods when they are ripe. Then my mother and my sisters and I take them to the market to sell.

Although they are only little seedpods, there are lots of things you can do with carobs. People buy the pods to dye clothes and make cosmetics from them. Farmers buy them to feed their pigs and cooks use them to flavour food and make sweets. Although it's fun to nibble the pods and suck out the sweet syrup from them, I would hate to have nothing else to eat! Only the very poorest people use carob pods for food.

But whenever I nibble one I remember the story my grandmother told me of a young man in a faraway country, who was so hungry he longed to eat the pods the pigs were gobbling up. It's one of the stories Jesus told.

25
Welcome Home, Son!

A man had two sons. One day the younger asked his father for his share of the family money so he could leave home. His father gave him lots of money, but the son was foolish. He went far away to a foreign country and spent all the money on wild living.

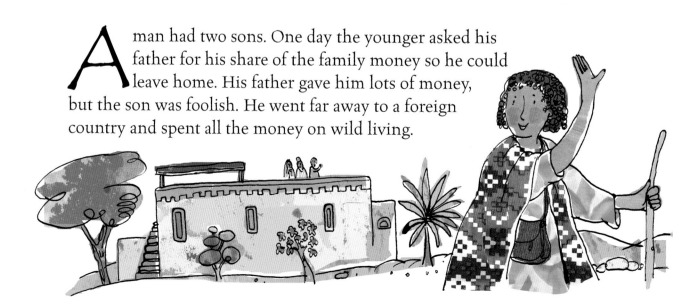

Famine struck the land and food was so scarce that he had to take a job feeding pigs. He was so hungry that even the pigs were better fed and he longed to eat their food.

'This is awful!' he said to himself. 'Perhaps if I go home and tell my father how sorry I am, he'll give me a job on the farm.'

So he set off for home. Before he even got there, his father saw him coming and rushed out to welcome him back. He hugged and kissed his son, full of love and joy that he had returned safely at last.

'Throw away these rags and bring my son some new clothes and shoes!' he said to the servants. 'Prepare the finest food because we're going to have a party to celebrate!'

When the older brother heard about this he was really jealous and went and complained to his father.

'It's not fair!' he said bitterly. 'I've been working hard for years and you've never thrown a party for me, while all my brother has done is to waste all your money!'

'You are always with me, son and everything I have is yours', said the father. 'So please be happy for him and celebrate with me because your brother has come back from the dead.'

Jesus always ended his story by saying, 'In the same way, God celebrates and welcomes every sinner who says he is sorry and returns to him.'

DORCAS'S STORY

My name is Dorcas and I live near the town of Capernaum. I'm going to tell you what happened when my brother Sam met Jesus. We were all going to the market-place to buy food and get some water. On the way we loaded the donkey up with firewood we found by the road. Then we went down to the well so that Mother could fill our big jug with water. Sam insisted on leading our strong, stubborn donkey, even though he is really too little.

He couldn't stop the donkey pulling him closer to a crowd of people who were listening to a man talking. A few seconds later Sam fell in a heap at the man's feet. I thought he would shout at Sam for interfering in men's business and I was scared. But, calling to his friends to grab the runaway donkey, he picked Sam up and sat him on his knee.

'My name's Jesus,' he said. 'You must be Sam.'

He was obviously an important man, but his shining eyes were kind and he let Sam sit there while he told a story. Afterwards Jesus gently put Sam down and waved goodbye.

26
Who's the Greatest?

The disciples came to Jesus to ask who would be the greatest person in the kingdom of heaven. Jesus picked up a child and showed him to them.

'Look at this little boy', Jesus said. 'Unless you turn from your sins and become like this child, you will never get into heaven. So anyone who makes himself as unimportant as a little child will be the greatest in heaven. Welcoming and caring for children and unimportant people is just as important as welcoming and caring for me. It would be better for you to tie a rock round your neck and jump into the sea than to make a little child like this do wicked things.

'You must never push away children like him. They're just as important as any grown-up. Remember, there are angels in heaven who look after children.'

MESHA'S STORY

My name is Mesha and I live in Kir-moab. My family all work with wool from the sheep that graze nearby. My father and my uncles shear the sheep and my aunts spin the wool. My mother looks after all the children. I have a brother, three sisters and eleven cousins, so she has quite a job!

Often my brother and I hide when she calls us to come inside, so we can keep on playing. Or sometimes one of the younger ones wanders off to look at the sheep. You'd think my mother wouldn't notice when there are sixteen of us to care for. But she always does! I'm sure that even if there were one hundred of us, like the sheep in the story Jesus told, she would always notice and look out for us. Jesus told this story to his disciples to show that he loved his people even more than a shepherd cares for his sheep.

27
The Lost Sheep

Once a shepherd had a hundred sheep. One night he counted them and there were only ninety-nine there. So he left the ninety-nine eating grass and went to look for the lost sheep. He searched and searched for hours. At last he saw a bit of white wool under some bushes. He lifted up the bushes and saw the little lost sheep. He cut away some of the branches so he could get it out, then he carefully carried it back to the other sheep. He sang all the way home because he was so happy to have found the lost sheep.

ESTHER'S STORY

My name is Esther and I live in Bethany. My father grows flax plants then Mother spins the flax into threads and finally weaves it into linen clothes. When someone dies their family come to our house to buy special cloths to wrap round the dead person. It is always a sad time, but Mother is proud that these grave clothes are made of the beautiful white linen she weaves.

When our neighbour Lazarus died Mother said to me, 'Here's some of my very best linen, Esther. Take it to Martha and Mary for me right away and tell them I will come to mourn with them soon.'

I took the cloth to the sisters and they wrapped their poor brother up, weeping all the time that their friend Jesus hadn't been able to get there in time to save him. You won't believe what happened next!

28
Bringing Lazarus Back to Life

Mary and Martha sent a message to Jesus telling him that their brother Lazarus was ill. Jesus was a friend of the family, but he did not come right away because he knew what was going to happen. He knew that what he would do for Lazarus would bring glory to God.

A few days later he said to his disciples, 'We must go to Judea now and see Lazarus.'

'But it's dangerous there!' said his disciples. 'Only a few days ago the Jewish leaders in Judea were trying to kill you!'

'But Lazarus is asleep now', said Jesus. 'I must go and wake him up.'

'He must be getting better then, if he's having a good sleep!' they replied.

'Lazarus is dead and for your sake I'm glad I wasn't there because this will give you another chance to believe in me.'

When they got there they met Martha and discovered that Lazarus had been dead and buried for four days.

'If only you'd been here', wept Martha, 'Lazarus would not have died!'

'He will rise again', said Jesus. 'I am the resurrection and the life. If anyone trusts in me he will rise again and live for ever.'

Martha found her sister Mary and told her Jesus had arrived. Mary too wept and told Jesus, 'Lazarus would not have died if you had been here!'

Jesus was upset at their sorrow and cried with them. Then they took him to the tomb of Lazarus, which was a cave with a big stone in front of it. Jesus told them to remove the stone.

'But he's been dead for four days!' said Martha. 'The smell will be terrible in this heat!'

'Just trust in me', said Jesus.

They rolled the stone away and Jesus prayed to God.

'Thank you, Father, for hearing my prayer and giving these people a chance to see your glory.'

Then he called into the tomb, 'Come out, Lazarus!'

The crowds that had gathered fell silent as the figure of Lazarus, wrapped in white linen grave clothes, came out of the tomb.

'Lazarus is fit and well once more', said Jesus. 'Let's unwrap these grave clothes and release him.'

BART'S STORY

My name's Bart and my father looks after our master's orchard of fruit trees. That's probably why I'm so good at climbing trees. I've got a story to tell. It was the day I climbed right to the top of the tall sycamore tree.

'I don't believe you!' said my friend Thomas, when I told him. 'That tree is the highest in Jericho!'

'Just ask Zacchaeus if you don't believe me! He climbed up the tree too.'

'Zacchaeus the tax collector?' said Thomas. 'My father says he's a liar and a cheat, so who'd believe anything he said! Besides, he's a grown-up, even though he's so small! What would he be doing up a tree?'

'He climbed up to see Jesus,' I replied. 'And he's a changed man now because of him! I heard everything they said to each other.'

29
Little Man up a Tree

One day Jesus went to Jericho, the home of Zacchaeus, the rich tax collector. He'd heard all about Jesus and wanted to see him for himself. But the crowds around Jesus were so large, and Zacchaeus was so short, that he couldn't see a thing. He ran along ahead and climbed to the top of a big sycamore tree to get a good view of the famous teacher as he went past.

As the crowd passed by underneath, Jesus stopped and looked up into the branches. Zacchaeus couldn't believe it when he heard his own name.

'Come down, Zacchaeus', said Jesus. 'I'd like to be a guest in your house today!'

Zacchaeus came down quickly and greeted Jesus with great joy.

'I'd be honoured if you came to eat with me', he said, and led the way to his house.

The crowds were not nearly as pleased as Zacchaeus.

'Why is the Lord going to eat with him?' they grumbled. 'Doesn't Jesus know Zacchaeus is an awful sinner, who always cheats us out of all our money!'

But at his house, Zacchaeus was telling Jesus how meeting him had changed him.

'I'm going to give half of all my riches to the poor!' said Zacchaeus. 'And if I've cheated anybody I will give them back four times what I took from them!'

Jesus was very pleased to hear this.

'You are just the sort of person I have come to help, Zacchaeus!' he said. 'Today you have been saved.'

ABI'S STORY

My name is Abi and I help my father, who's a doctor here in Jericho. I look after the garden where we grow the plants and herbs he uses to make medicines. I've learnt that rue is good for cleaning wounds and the tall hyssop is used for treating the plague.

But there are some conditions that even my father can do nothing about. There are many blind people in our town and there is no hope of my father curing them. My friend Zibiah's father is a blind beggar called Bartimaeus. She leads him about so he can beg for money to buy them a little food. We both thought he would always be blind and always need to beg for food.

But he met Jesus on the road one day and now he has been cured, and even has a job! This is the story Zibiah told me.

30
I Can See Again!

Jesus had been teaching in Jericho. As he and his disciples left the city, a huge crowd followed them.

'Who's that going by?' asked a blind beggar called Bartimaeus, who was sitting by the side of the road. 'He must be important for people to be calling out to him so loudly!'

'It's Jesus of Nazareth,' they told him. 'The prophet who is healing people and teaching about the love of God.'

Bartimaeus had heard about Jesus and his miracles and believed that he was the Son of God.

'Have mercy on me, Jesus!' he called out, hoping Jesus would hear him amidst the noisy crowd.

'Be quiet, Bartimaeus!' some of the people yelled at him. 'The Lord has more important things to do than to listen to a dirty old blind beggar!'

But Bartimaeus shouted even louder, 'Have mercy on me, Jesus!'

When Jesus heard him he stopped in the road and said, 'Tell that man to come here to me.'

So they called out to the blind man, 'Come on, you're a lucky guy. He's calling for you!'

Bartimaeus ripped off his dirty old coat and flung it aside. He stumbled down the road towards Jesus.

'What do you want me to do?' asked Jesus kindly, when Bartimaeus reached him.

'I believe you can give me back my sight!' said Bartimaeus. 'I want to see again!'

'You believed in me, so I will do it,' said Jesus. 'Your faith has healed you.'

'I can see again!' exclaimed the blind man immediately, and followed Jesus down the road.

SIMEON'S STORY

My name is Simeon and my father sells donkeys. But I have my own donkey too. One day something very exciting happened, which made me late meeting my mother.

'Where have you been, Simeon?' said my mother.

'Some men came and borrowed our colt, Mother, and I had to go with them to make sure he was all right!' I said.

'Who borrowed him and why?' she asked.

'He was tied up outside as usual, and two men tried to take him for their master to ride on!' I said. 'I told them he'd never been ridden and ran for Father, but he said they could borrow him! Then the king rode him into Jerusalem . . .'

'What king?' asked Mother. 'Why don't you start again at the beginning, Simeon!'

31
The Proud Donkey

Jesus was on his way to Jerusalem. He told two of his disciples to go on ahead and borrow a young colt.

'As you go into the village you'll see a young donkey tied up outside a house,' said Jesus. 'Untie it and bring it to me. If anyone objects, tell them that the Master needs it.'

The disciples soon found the donkey. They repeated what Jesus had said and were allowed to borrow the donkey. They led it up to Jesus at the Mount of Olives and folded their cloaks carefully on its back to make a soft saddle. Jesus mounted the donkey, which carried him easily.

Followed by the disciples, they headed up the track towards the big city of Jerusalem. Alongside the path the people gathered, chattering excitedly.

'That's Jesus who raised Lazarus from the dead!'

'Lazarus? You mean Mary and Martha's brother Lazarus from Bethany, just down the road?' said one man.

'That's right. Lazarus was dead and buried for four days and Jesus brought him back to life!'

The man looked amazed and stared at the Lord riding by so quietly. Then he started to cheer. The Lord stopped at the top of the hill and looked at Jerusalem below. Laughing, cheering people lined the road all the way to the city. The donkey stepped carefully down the steep slope. Proudly he carried the Lord into his city like a king. Children ran to the palm trees growing beside the road and started pulling off the low branches. They waved them like flags as Jesus passed by. Then everybody threw loads of palm leaves on the dusty path in front of the donkey, as they do if a king rides by. Some people even laid their cloaks at his feet. The people all clapped as they passed by, shouting and cheering.

'God bless the King!'

'Hosanna!'

'Blessed is he who comes in the name of the Lord!'

Everyone was delighted to see Jesus ride past, until they got to Jerusalem. There were still hundreds of people fluttering palms and cheering, but there were other groups looking very angry at the way Jesus was being greeted.

'Just look at the long faces of those Pharisees!' said one of the Lord's followers. 'They hate to see how popular Jesus is with the people.'

The Pharisees were a group of people who kept the rules of the Jewish law very strictly. Jesus knew that many of these laws were no longer important. He would do things that broke the law, like healing people on the Sabbath, and this made the Pharisees angry. Some of them came forward and said to the Lord, 'Tell your followers not to shout like this!'

'If the people kept quiet, the very stones my donkey is treading on would burst out cheering!' said Jesus and continued on his kingly ride into Jerusalem.

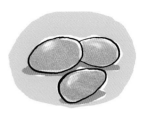

MARTHA'S STORY

My name is Martha and I work with my mother, who's a cook. Today we walked miles so she could cook a special Passover meal for Jesus. My feet ache and all the dirt from the roads has covered my toes. When Jesus's friends get here, a servant will wash their feet, so they'll feel comfortable before their meal. I'm so glad that's not my job!

'The food's ready, Martha!' says my mother. 'Help me carry it to the table.'

I carry in the hard boiled eggs carefully. What I see nearly makes me drop them!

32
Dirty Feet

Jesus and his followers arrived at the house to share the Passover meal. Jesus took off his coat, poured water into a bowl and tied a towel round his waist. He knelt on the floor and started to wash John's feet.

'You're next, Peter!' he said to the big fisherman.

'I'll never let you wash my feet, Lord!' Peter protested.

'But if I don't wash your feet, that means you won't really belong to me,' said Jesus.

'If that's how it is, Lord, then don't just wash my feet!' said Peter. 'Wash my head and my hands as well!'

'Now, Peter, I know you had a bath before you came out, so your body must be clean,' said Jesus as he washed Peter's dusty feet. 'All but one of you are clean. It's just your feet that are dirty from the walk here.'

Peter didn't understand why Jesus was acting like a servant. 'Why are you doing this, Lord?' he asked.

'You have called me Lord and Master and that is only right because that is what I am', said Jesus. 'Since your Lord and Master can wash your feet, so you must wash each other's feet and the servants' feet too. You mustn't think yourselves better than the servants any more because I have made all men equal. You must do what I have done in all things, not just washing feet. You must act humbly and be kind to everyone. This way you will be blessed.'

DAVID'S STORY

My name is David. I'm the son of a water seller. Poor people like us have to fetch our own water from the well. My mother does this every day, carrying the water home in a big pot balanced on her head. But rich people can pay to have their water carried to them and this is my father's job.

Once, two men called Peter and John followed him to a house where the master had ordered some fresh water.

'Jesus told us you would lead us to a house with a big upstairs room where we can prepare to celebrate the Passover feast with him,' they said to my father.

How on earth did Jesus know that he would be carrying water there at just that moment? Father was curious about Jesus and asked one of the servants what happened at the feast. This is what he told him.

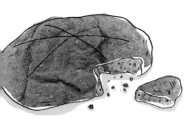

33
The Last Supper

In the evening Jesus and his twelve disciples came to eat the Passover feast together in the room upstairs. While they were eating, Jesus said sadly, 'One of you sitting here eating with me will betray me and give me up to be killed.'

Everyone was filled with sorrow and they asked him, 'Is it me, Lord?'

Jesus gave Judas a piece of bread and said, 'God has decided what will happen to me, but this is the man who will betray me.'

But nobody understood what he meant. Then Jesus took some more bread. He gave thanks to God, broke it into little pieces and gave it to his friends, saying, 'Eat this, for it is my body.'

Then he took a cup of wine. He gave thanks and gave them each a drink. 'Drink this, for it is my blood which must be shed so that many can be forgiven. I will not drink wine again until I drink a far better kind in the kingdom of God. Do these things to remember me when I am gone.'

Then they sang a hymn together and went up to the Mount of Olives to pray.

JONATHAN'S STORY

My name's Jonathan and I help Malchus, a servant of Caiaphas, who is the chief priest in Jerusalem. Tonight Malchus told me to go with the soldiers to carry extra torches. He said that Jesus claims to be the Messiah, God's son, the one we've all been waiting for, for thousands of years! That's why they're arresting him. He's just a man. How can he be God's son? I listened to the men talking as we walked.

'How will we know which one is Jesus?' asked Malchus.

'I'm Judas,' said one of the men. 'I've been his disciple for ages and he trusts me. He's in the garden at Gethsemane tonight, praying with the rest of his disciples. When we get there, I'll go and kiss him. That's the signal. Then you get him!'

It didn't seem right to me, a man wanting to betray his own friend like that. But I'd heard they were giving Judas lots of money for it. No wonder he looked so pleased with himself.

I thought Jesus would have a whole army with him but there was no army. Just one sad-looking man, kneeling in prayer, and a small group stretched out beneath the olive trees, fast asleep.

34
Malchus and his Miracle Ear

Every man was well armed with swords and clubs when they went to arrest Jesus, who was praying in the garden at Gethsemane. His sleeping disciples leapt up, rubbing their eyes, when they heard the soldiers.

'Who are you looking for?' Jesus asked.

Judas went up to him and kissed him on the cheek in greeting, the way men do when they meet their friends.

'Hello, teacher', he said.

'Judas', said Jesus sadly. 'How can you betray the Messiah with a kiss?'

Suddenly the soldiers pounced on Jesus and arrested him.

Immediately, one of his disciples came rushing at Malchus with a sword. Malchus yelled and blood poured down his neck. He gazed with horror at his ear, lying on the ground at his feet in an ever-growing pool of blood.

'Put your sword away!' ordered Jesus. 'Violence isn't the answer! I could just ask my Father to send down angels to protect me, if I wanted to. But I must do what is planned for me so that everyone will know I am the Son of God.'

Then he reached down and picked up the ear from the ground. Very gently Jesus put it back in place.

'The pain's gone!' said Malchus in amazement.

There was blood on his clothes and on the ground. But there was none on his head. His ear looked as if it had never been cut off at all. Jesus had healed him. The soldiers grabbed Jesus and took him away.

TIMOTHY'S STORY

I am Timothy and my father is a trader. Today he gave me a great present – a cockerel. He'll wake me up by crowing at daylight. I'm going to call my cockerel Peter because he reminds me of a story my father told me. It's about what happened just after Jesus shared his last supper with the disciples, when he told them that they were all going to desert him.

35
I Don't Know Him!

Jesus was arrested in the Garden of Gethsemane and taken away by the soldiers. Peter followed behind them into the courtyard of the high priest and warmed himself at the fire there, while the chief priests and elders questioned Jesus.

One of the high priest's maids came into the courtyard and saw Peter sitting there. 'Weren't you with that man Jesus, from Galilee?' she said.

'I don't know what you're talking about!' said Peter, and quickly went out to the gateway.

Just then, a cockerel crowed.

When the maid caught sight of Peter again, she pointed him out to the people around, 'Look at that man!

72

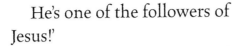

He's one of the followers of Jesus!'

'Not me!' said Peter, and turned away to talk to another man. A little while later someone said, 'I'm sure you're one of Jesus' men. Your accent shows you are a man of Galilee, just like him!'

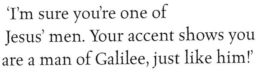

'I don't know Jesus!' said Peter firmly.

Then the cockerel crowed for the second time and Peter remembered that Jesus had said, 'Before the cock crows for the second time tomorrow, three times you will pretend you never knew me!'

Peter realised what he had done and went away crying bitter tears of shame and grief.

TABITHA'S STORY

I'm Tabitha and my father is a saddle maker. This is a story I told my brother and sister when they were playing kings and queens. They were fighting over the crown of buttercups I had made them.

'It's a beautiful crown,' I said, 'not like the thorny crown the soldiers made Jesus wear when they dressed him as a king to make fun of him. Give Deborah back her crown, Jem and I will make another one for you. While I do that I will tell you the story of how Jesus died. He knew he had to die, so it's a sad story, but it has a wonderful ending!'

36
The Crucifixion

After Jesus was arrested, they brought him to Pontius Pilate, the Roman governor. He didn't think Jesus had committed any crime, but the people wanted Jesus to die. Pontius Pilate was worried that if the crowds rioted, he might lose his job, so he let the soldiers take Jesus to be crucified.

The soldiers made fun of Jesus. They dressed him in a purple cloak and made a crown out of thorny twigs with sharp spikes.

'We're worshipping the king of the Jews,' they mocked and then they beat him harshly. They tried to make him carry his heavy cross to the place where they were going to kill him, but they had hurt him so much that he could not do it. They had to get a passer-by to take it instead. They fixed Jesus to the cross by hammering nails into his hands and feet and then they shared out his clothes amongst themselves.

Even though they had been so cruel to him, Jesus called out to his Father in heaven, 'Father, forgive them, for they don't understand what they're doing.'

Two criminals were also being crucified with him. One of them asked for forgiveness too and Jesus promised that he would go to heaven with him that very day.

Jesus's friend John looked after Mary, who was filled with grief because her son was being killed. At noon the sky got very dark. Three hours later Jesus called out, 'My work is finished now! I give my spirit to you, Father!' and then he died. At that moment an earthquake shook the ground. In the Temple, the curtain tore open, showing that the barrier between the people and God had now been removed.

In the evening a rich man called Joseph of Arimathea asked Pontius Pilate if he could have Jesus's body. He was a good man, who believed in Jesus. He wrapped the body in fine linen cloths and took it to a tomb that had been carved in the rocks on the side of a hill. Then he got his servants to roll a huge stone to cover up the entrance to the tomb.

RUTH'S STORY

I'm Ruth, the spice merchant's daughter, and I can remember what happened after Jesus was crucified. My father was still selling spices to people in his shop, as if nothing extraordinary had happened. I dropped the basket of dates and figs I had been sent to buy and yelled at the top of my voice, 'Jesus is alive!'

'What nonsense, Ruth!' said my father. 'You know they crucified the Lord! You were here yesterday when Salome and her friends came to buy spices and oils to anoint his dead body.'

'I've just met Salome and she told me all about it,' I said. 'They went to the tomb with the spices and they saw the most unbelievable thing!'

37
Jesus is Alive Again!

Very early in the morning the women went to the tomb where the body of Jesus had been laid. Mary Magdalene, James's mother, Mary, and Salome carried spices they had brought to anoint him.

'How are we going to get into the tomb?' they asked each other in worried voices. 'That stone Joseph put there is too heavy for us to move and the gardeners won't be here to help us this early.'

But when they reached the tomb they found that the heavy stone had been rolled away and they could walk right into the cave. But the stone shelf where the dead body of Jesus should have been lying was empty, apart from some folded cloths. Jesus was gone!

Then they saw that there was someone else there. A man dressed in dazzling white clothes was sitting nearby. They were terrified and crouched down in fear.

'Don't be afraid!' he said to them. 'I know you are looking for Jesus of Nazareth. But why look for him here, in the place of the dead? He isn't here. He has risen from the dead, just as he said he would. Jesus is alive again! He has gone on ahead of you to Galilee, but don't worry, he'll meet you there. But first go back and tell Peter and the rest of the disciples that Jesus is risen!'

The women were amazed and shocked, but full of joy. They ran back to tell their friends, who could hardly believe what had happened. Peter and John raced ahead to see if it was true. John ran faster and got there first, but he was afraid to go in and look.

But Peter ran straight in and saw the empty shelf where the folded grave clothes lay. John finally followed him and they both stared with surprise. It was true. Jesus was gone. He really was alive again!

BENJAMIN'S STORY

My name's Benjamin and I'm going to be a gardener when I grow up, just like my father and my grandfather and his father before him. My grandfather worked for Joseph of Arimathea and tended his gardens, including the one that held the tomb where they put the body of Jesus. Grandfather was one of the four men who rolled the huge stone in front of the cave. But he was still at home next morning when the women came and found the tomb empty.

He always says he wishes he'd been there to see it and didn't just hear the story afterwards. I wish I'd been there too!

38
The First Appearance

The women had been amazed when they went to Jesus's tomb and found it empty. After she'd told Peter and the disciples what had happened, Mary Magdalene went back to the empty tomb, feeling very confused. She took another look inside and started to cry again. Two angels were inside the tomb and they spoke to her kindly.

'Why are you crying?' they asked.

'They have taken the Master's body away and I don't know where they have put it!' she sobbed.

She turned around and saw another man.

'Why are you crying?' he said. 'Are you looking for someone?'

She thought the man must be a gardener.

Perhaps he knew what had happened to Jesus.

'Please, sir,' she said, 'if you've taken his body away, just tell me where it is, so I can go and get it.'

'Mary!' said a voice she recognised very well.

'Master!' she gasped and reached out to hug him.

'You cannot touch me yet because I still have to go home to my Father. But go and tell the others you have seen me,' said Jesus.

Immediately she ran back to find the disciples to tell them the news.

JOSEPH'S STORY

My name is Joseph. My father is a scribe and sometimes he has to walk miles to write a letter for someone. Last week he had to go all the way to Emmaus, carrying a great roll of papyrus on his back.

'Why does he have to go so far?' grumbled my brother Obal. 'Don't they have scribes in Emmaus?'

'Cleopas asked for Father specially,' I said. 'He wanted his account of the story written down as soon as possible, so he doesn't forget anything that happened. But if I'd met a dead man on the road, I'd never forget a single detail!'

'A dead man?' asked Obal. 'What are you talking about?'

'Cleopas and his friend met Jesus on the road, after he was dead and buried!' I replied. 'He was so excited he ran all the way back to Jerusalem to tell people about it! It was seven miles!'

39
On the Rocky Road to Emmaus

Cleopas and his friend left Jerusalem and walked towards their homes in Emmaus. They could talk about nothing but the strange things that had happened earlier in the day, when the women found the empty tomb. They met a man on the road, who joined them as they walked, still talking about the death of Jesus.

'You seem to be deep in conversation,' said the stranger. 'What is worrying you?'

'You must be the only man in Jerusalem who hasn't heard the terrible things that have happened to Jesus!' said Cleopas. 'Even though he was the Messiah who had come to save Israel, they arrested him and crucified him three days ago. Some of our women went to his tomb this morning and ran back to us all with some strange tale that his body had disappeared! Two of the men went to have a look and, sure enough, the body was gone! What do you think of that?'

'If only you had all believed what the Scriptures taught you!' said the man. 'They told you that the Messiah would have to suffer and die before he came to glory.'

Then he explained all the things that the Scriptures had said and what they really meant. By this time they were nearing Emmaus.

'Why don't you come home with me, stranger?' said Cleopas. 'It's a long rocky road from Jerusalem and you must be tired. Come and eat with us and spend the night at my house before continuing on your journey.'

The stranger agreed and went home with them. Before they began to eat their evening meal, the man gave thanks for the food. Then he split open a small loaf and passed it around. God had kept them from recognising the man before, but now it was as if he opened their eyes and they realised that the man was Jesus. But as quickly as they had seen him, Jesus disappeared before their eyes.

'That explains why we felt so excited and cheered up when he was explaining the Scriptures!' said Cleopas. 'We must go back to Jerusalem and tell the others!'

KEZIA'S STORY

I'm Kezia. I'm a dancer and I wander around the country with my family, performing in houses and market-places. I tell stories too. When I was in North Africa I worked with an elephant called Juju. People here are amazed when I tell them that. Today a boy, about my own age, yelled, 'What a load of rubbish! A beast as high as a house, with a nose so long and strong that it can pick you up! I do not believe it!'

'Is your name Thomas, by any chance?' I asked. 'For you're a real doubting Thomas!'

Nobody in the crowd seemed to recognise the story of Doubting Thomas. This is it.

40
I Don't Believe It!

Three days after he had died, Cleopas and his friend had just seen Jesus walking down the road, even though he was supposed to be dead. They ran all the way back to Jerusalem to tell the disciples the news. The disciples were in a locked room, hiding from the Jewish authorities. Cleopas banged on the door and Peter let them in and locked the door again.

'We've seen Jesus! He's alive again . . . ' began Cleopas.

Suddenly Jesus himself was in the room with them, although the door had not been unlocked again. They were frightened at first, but then pleased and excited to see him.

'Don't you believe it's me?' Jesus asked them. 'Touch me if you think I'm a ghost! Feel the holes in my hands and feet where they banged in the nails.'

They gave him a piece of fish from their supper and he ate it, which proved to everyone that he was really alive again.

'The Father sent me here to teach you everything I can. Now it is your turn', said Jesus. 'I am sending you out to teach the rest of the people. If you forgive people's sins they will be forgiven. But wait here in the city until the power of the Holy Spirit comes upon you.'

Then Jesus blessed them and disappeared again.

One of the disciples, called Thomas, was not in the room when this had happened. When he heard the news he just couldn't believe it.

'I won't believe it until I see Jesus for myself!' said Thomas. 'I'd have to stick my

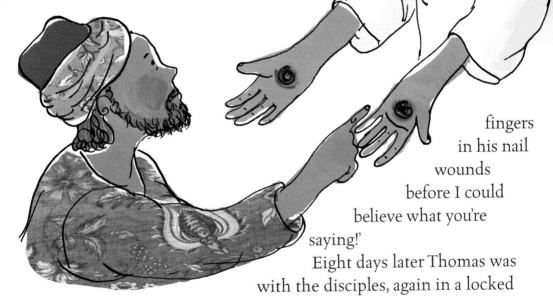

fingers in his nail wounds before I could believe what you're saying!'

Eight days later Thomas was with the disciples, again in a locked room, when Jesus appeared once more.

'Put your fingers into these nail holes in my hands!' Jesus said to Thomas. 'Stop doubting and believe the evidence of your own eyes and hands.'

Thomas knelt down before him. 'My Lord and my God!' he said.

'You believe it now that you see it, Thomas', said Jesus. 'Blessed are those who believe, even though they have never seen me.'

JAMES'S STORY

I am James and I sell fish. Grandfather is a fisherman and he often says, 'Fishing is not what it used to be.'

'What does he mean, James?' muttered my friend Bo, as we helped Grandfather and my older brothers unload their catch. 'There's masses of fish there!'

'He's talking about the days when he was our age and Jesus made sure the disciples' boats were so full of fish they nearly sank!' I said. 'Grandfather saw it with his own eyes! Once Jesus barbecued fish for them on the beach after a big catch. Grandfather helped in one of the disciples' boats, so he heard it all. I remember it particularly because Grandfather had to explain to me that when Jesus said, "Feed my lambs," he didn't really mean lambs, but Jesus often taught people in stories.'

'What did he mean then?' asked Bo, puzzled by this talk of lambs amidst all the fish.

'I think he meant teach them and look after them,' I said. 'Lambs must be children and sheep grown-ups!'

41
Feed my Sheep

One night some of the disciples went fishing with Peter. They fished until dawn, but they caught nothing. A man on the beach called out to them, 'Have you caught anything yet?'

'Nothing at all!' Peter called back.

'Throw out your nets on the other side of the boat and you'll have a fine catch!' said the man.

They cast their nets on the right-hand side of the boat and immediately the nets were so full of fish that it was impossible to heave them on to the boat.

'That was Jesus!' exclaimed John.

Peter jumped over the side and waded towards Jesus and the others followed in the boat, pulling their bulging nets behind them. There were one hundred and fifty-three fish in just one net. Jesus had already started a fire and was soon busy cooking for them.

'Put some more fish on the fire and come and join me for breakfast,' he said, offering them the fish he had already cooked. This was the third time he had appeared to his disciples after his death.

After breakfast he said to Peter, 'Do you love me, Peter?'

'Of course I do!' said Peter.

'Feed my lambs!' said Jesus. 'Do you really love me?' Jesus asked again.

'You know I do!' said Peter.

'Tend my sheep!' said Jesus.

He repeated his question again and asked Peter to feed his sheep. Then he said, 'When you were young you could do as you pleased. But now people need you and people will make you go where you do not want to go.

Follow me, Peter.'

ANDREW'S STORY

My name's Andrew and my family have been growing olives here for generations. Everyone knows they are the finest olives in Israel and that our olive grove is the place where Jesus chose to leave the earth to return to his Father in heaven. Sometimes I take my friends right to the top of the hill to show them the exact spot.

42
The First Easter

In the forty days after he died, Jesus appeared to the disciples many times. He reassured them that he was truly alive once more and taught them about the kingdom of God. But they always had more questions for him.

One day Jesus met them on the Mount of Olives. The disciples were all longing for the Romans, who had conquered and ruled Israel, to be thrown out of their country.

'When will you give our country back to the people?' they asked.

'You don't need to worry about times and dates', said Jesus. 'Just wait here and soon I will send you the Holy Spirit. He will give you the power to tell the whole world about me. It is important for you to teach them why I died and came back to life.'

When Jesus had said this, a cloud appeared on the mountainside and hid him from their sight. They all looked up into the sky, straining their eyes to see him. Suddenly two angels, dressed all in white, appeared beside them.

'Why are you looking for Jesus up there in the sky?' they asked. 'He has been taken up into heaven and one day he will return to earth in the same way.'

JASON'S STORY

I'm Jason, the son of a yoghurt maker. I saw something fantastic at the Temple today!

'Wherever have you been, Jason?' my mother asked. 'And what's all the shouting in the Temple courtyard? I could hear it from here, but I couldn't leave the stall to find out.'

'Do you know that lame beggar who sits outside the temple?' I said, breathlessly. 'The one with really twisted ankles?'

'I know the one,' said Mother. 'Two men carry him down to the Beautiful Gate every day to beg. Sometimes I take him a bowl of my best yoghurt because he has so little to eat. What about him?'

'A miracle happened to him, Mother, and I saw it! Peter and John were there and Peter healed him in the name of Jesus, their dead master.'

43
Peter Heals the Beggar

Every day a poor lame beggar was carried to the Beautiful Gate to beg money from people going into the Temple. One day Peter and John passed by as they went in to pray at nine o'clock. He called out to them, 'Could you spare a small coin, good sirs?'

Peter said, 'Take a good look at us.'

The beggar did so willingly, hoping for some money.

'I haven't got any money,' said Peter. 'But I *do* have something valuable for you. In the name of Jesus Christ, I tell you to get up and walk!'

The lame man got an incredible feeling in his ankles and feet. Peter held out his hand and the beggar leapt to his feet.

'Look at me!' he yelled. 'Praise God, for he has healed me! I can walk at last!'

He didn't just walk though. He jumped and skipped and ran! Everyone turned to stare at him and shouted in amazement.

'It's the lame man from the gate!'

'He's never walked in his life!'

'Here, come and see the lame man walking! Peter has healed him!'

Soon crowds had gathered to watch the beggar leap and run. Peter said to them, 'Friends, why are you looking so amazed? Be sure that we couldn't do a miracle like this by ourselves. It's by the power of Jesus that this lame man has been healed.'

'Jesus?' asked one man. 'The man we told Pilate to kill?'

'The same holy man,' agreed Peter. 'All you people thought you'd put an end to his life. But God has brought him back to life and it is by his power that your lame friend can walk. Now you should all turn from your bad ways. Trust God and he will bless you.'

SIMON'S STORY

My name is Simon and I'm a gatekeeper's son. Our house is set into the city wall and it's my father's job to open one of the gates of the city of Damascus early in the morning and close and lock it up at night. I was there the day that Saul came to Damascus. We had heard much about him and were terrified. He was very dangerous to people like my family because he wanted to kill every Christian he found. But something happened that day which changed him completely.

I actually saw Saul coming into the city. But he was nothing like the monster I had imagined. He had to be led into Damascus, a blind and frightened man. Of course my father tried to find out what had happened to change Saul so much, and it's quite a story.

44
Heaven's Blinding Light

A young man from Tarsus, called Saul, was one of the worst enemies of the Christians. He was a strict Jew who liked to persecute Christians by getting them put in jail or even killed. Saul was convinced that the old Jewish law was right and Jesus was wrong, so he thought that by persecuting Christians he would please God. Saul got permission from the high priest to go to the city of Damascus to hunt out more Christians. He meant to bring them back to Jerusalem and throw them in prison.

Damascus was about five days' from from Jerusalem, so Saul set off on his journey. He was travelling along the road, when suddenly a blinding light flashed down from heaven. He fell to the ground with his hands over his eyes.

Then he heard a voice from heaven call out, 'Saul, why are you persecuting me?'

Saul was very frightened and said, 'Who are you, sir?'

'I am Jesus, the one you are persecuting!' said the voice. 'Now get up, go to the city and I will tell you what to do next.'

The men Saul was travelling with were amazed because they could hear the voice, but they could not see anyone. When Saul got up, he found that he was blind and the men had to lead him to Damascus. He stayed blind for three days, during which time he had nothing to eat or drink.

There was a Christian in Damascus called Ananias. God spoke to him and told him to go to a house on Straight Street where he would find a man called Saul. But Ananias had heard how cruel Saul was and he was frightened.

'Saul has come to Damascus to arrest all the Christians!' he said. 'I'm too scared to go near him!'

'I have chosen Saul to tell people about me,' said God. 'Go to him now.'

So Ananias went to the house. 'Hello, Saul,' he said. 'I've been sent by the Lord Jesus, who appeared to you on the road.'

Immediately something like fish scales fell from Saul's eyes and he could see again. He was filled with the power of the Holy Spirit, was baptised straight away and became a Christian. Then he was known by the Roman name of Paul.

Soon he was telling everyone the good news about Jesus Christ. After a while he had told so many people that the Jews tried to kill him. But Paul heard they were watching the gates of the city so they could capture him if he tried to leave. Some friends let him down in a basket from the high stone wall of the city and he escaped and was able to continue telling people about Jesus.

PHOEBE'S STORY

My name is Phoebe and I'm frightened for my big sister Rhoda and her friends because they are all followers of Jesus. King Herod has already had John's brother James put to death. We were all staying over at Mark's house, praying for Peter, who's been arrested. Suddenly there was a loud knocking on the door. Rhoda went to answer it and then came racing back.

'It's Peter at the door!' she shouted.

'Don't be ridiculous!' everyone said. 'Peter's in prison. You must be imagining it!'

'It's true!' Rhoda said firmly. 'I saw him through the window and I heard his voice!'

'They must have killed him then. You must have seen his ghost!'

'He has a very firm knock for a dead person,' said Mark's mother. 'I can still hear him!'

Rhoda gasped when she realised she hadn't even let Peter in! This is the story Peter told us about what happened before my sister left him standing on the doorstep!

45
Left Standing on the Doorstep

Peter had been arrested and thrown into prison. The night before his trial he was fast asleep, chained to two guards and guarded by sixteen soldiers. Suddenly he felt something shaking him. He opened his eyes, but could see nothing at first because the cell was filled with light. Then he realised there was an angel standing there.

'Get up!' said the angel. 'Put your sandals on, wrap your cloak round yourself and follow me!'

As Peter got up, his chains fell off and crashed to the floor. But it was as if nobody heard a thing! He followed the angel, passing all the guards on the way out. When they got to the heavy iron gate of the prison Peter wondered how the angel would get them through it. But it opened itself quietly in front of them. They walked along the street for a while and then the angel vanished into thin air.

Peter really thought he was dreaming. But then he realised at last that he was free and ran to the house of Mary, Mark's mother. He knew for certain that he was awake when he knocked at the door and Rhoda left him shivering on the doorstep!

Everyone was so happy that their prayers for Peter's freedom had been answered.

'You must all go out tomorrow and tell everyone how the angel freed me!' said Peter. 'Then they will realise the power of Jesus.'

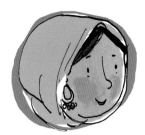

LYDIA'S STORY

My name is Lydia, and I'm the daughter of a dried fruit merchant. My story is about the slave girl who used to sit next to our stall in the market-place. I saw her every day while I helped Father sell fresh figs and dates. I would have liked to be friends, even though she was older than me. But she wasn't allowed to have friends. I didn't even know her name, but I knew she was always scared of her masters.

People would pay her to tell them what was going to happen in the future. But she was never allowed to keep any of the money for herself. One day I went to give her some dates and saw the most incredible thing happen.

46
The Fortune Teller

A slave girl sat in her usual place in the busy market. She saw a crowd of people following two men and went after them. Something made her keep calling out to everyone, 'These men are servants of God and have come to tell you how to have your sins forgiven!'

The two men were Paul and Silas. They travelled around the world, telling people the Good News – that God had sent his son, Jesus, to die for the sins of the world. They told people to say that they were sorry for the bad things they had done. If they were really sorry and believed that Jesus was God's son and had died for them, they would go to heaven. Lots of people gathered around to listen to this strange tale.

'Can it be true that all you have to do is to say you're sorry for your sins and then accept God's gift of everlasting life with him in heaven?' they asked.

The idea made everyone very excited. But the slave girl followed Paul and Silas around, shouting and disturbing their talks with fortune telling. God showed Paul that the poor slave girl had an evil demon inside her that made her do these things, even if she didn't want to. With God's power Paul called out to the demon.

'I command you, in the name of Jesus Christ, to come out of her!'

The demon came out immediately and left the slave girl, never to return. She was so happy to be free of the demon, but her masters were not. Now that the demon was gone, she couldn't tell fortunes any more. That meant she couldn't earn money for her cruel masters.

They blamed Paul and Silas for this. They dragged them to the judges in the market-place and told lies about what they had done. The judges believed the lies and Paul and Silas were beaten and thrown into prison.

RUHAMMAH'S STORY

My name is Ruhammah and my father is a charcoal maker. Charcoal is wood that has been covered up so no air can reach it, then burned very slowly. It is very useful because it burns with a flame that is hot enough for melting metals. When you think about burning, you always imagine flames, don't you? I was surprised when I first saw my father's charcoal pit. There are no flames to be seen at all because the wood is buried under layers of bracken, soil and turf. But underneath it is slowly burning away and making charcoal. My father has to watch over it all the time when it is burning, to make sure no air gets in.

But when the feast of Pentecost comes, even my father stops work to celebrate. He told me the story of how real fiery flames appeared over the heads of Jesus's disciples. It must be a miracle when you get flames with no fire.

47
Tongues of Fire

Seven weeks after Jesus was crucified and ten days after he was taken up into heaven, his disciples met to celebrate Pentecost. This was a Jewish festival, also called the Feast of Weeks, which was always celebrated on the fiftieth day after Passover. Suddenly the whole house was filled with a roaring sound, like a huge wind blowing in a fierce storm. The disciples looked at each other in amazement, because each of them had a tongue of fire resting above his head. It looked like a huge candle flame. They began to praise God with great joy. The Holy Spirit came down upon them and made them able to speak in many different languages.

There were many Jews about, from all over the world, who had come to celebrate Pentecost in Jerusalem. When they heard the roaring in the sky above the house, they all rushed over to see what was happening. They were amazed to hear their own languages being spoken by the disciples, who had never even been to their lands.

'Aren't these men from Galilee?' asked one man. 'I'm from Rome, yet they are praising their God in my language!'

'And I'm an Egyptian!' said another. 'But I can understand them perfectly!'

With the disciples praising God in dozens of languages, it was very noisy indeed. Some people began to wonder if they were drunk.

'How can we be drunk? It's only nine o'clock in the morning!' said Peter. 'God has poured out his Holy Spirit upon us. Now we'll be able to perform miracles like Jesus did! We'll have visions and dreams and be able to tell people what God wants them to do; just as the prophet Joel said we would, in the Scriptures. Jesus was crucified, but now he is alive and God has made him Lord of all!'

When they heard this, the crowd was ashamed and asked what they should do.

'All you have to do is tell God you are sorry for the bad things you've done and be baptised,' said Peter. 'Then God will forgive your sins and give you the gift of the Holy Spirit too!'

On that morning three thousand people became Christians. After that they met frequently and shared everything they had. The disciples performed many miracles and more and more people became believers.

PHILIP'S STORY

I am Philip, the jailor's son. Today everyone has been asking me what happened at the jail last night. I was there, so I know. Paul and Silas had been wrongly arrested, Father knew that, but he still had to do his job.

'The judges say they'll kill me if these two escape!' my father told me. 'So I'm taking no chances. I'll chain their legs to this iron ring, down here in the deepest dungeon. They'll never get out!'

When we went to bed last night, we never dreamt what would happen.

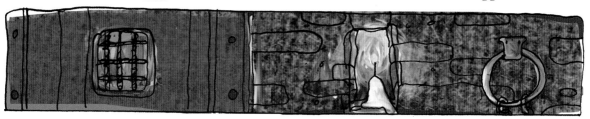

48
Freed by an Earthquake

At midnight Paul and Silas were still praying and singing joyful hymns to God. The other prisoners were amazed that Paul and Silas could be so happy when they were in prison. This Jesus must be a very special person to make them behave like that. They listened eagerly as Paul told them the stories Jesus had told.

At midnight a frightening thing happened! The walls shook, the bars rattled, all the doors opened and the chains of every prisoner fell off! It was an earthquake! When the jailer came running in and saw all the doors open he was horrified.

'They said they'd kill me if those prisoners escaped!' he moaned. 'All the doors are open so they must have gone. I'd be better killing myself now than letting them torture me tomorrow when they find out!'

He drew his sword to kill himself, but dropped it in amazement when Paul called out, 'Don't do it! We're all still here!'

When the jailer saw them, he realised that God must have sent the earthquake to free them. He fell down on his knees.

'Tell me what I must do to be saved!' he begged.

'Trust and believe in the Lord Jesus and you and your whole family will be saved', said Paul.

When he told them about Jesus they were filled with joy and asked to be baptised. They all celebrated with a big meal, even though it was the middle of the night, and they were still in the prison next morning when the judges sent a message to tell Paul and Silas to leave.

'We've been beaten and thrown into prison without a trial, even though we're Roman citizens', said Paul. 'If they want us to go they must come and set us free themselves.'

The judges were worried when they heard that they'd locked up such important people. It quickly made them change their minds, as they could lose their own lives for doing such a thing. So they rushed down to the prison and begged Paul and Silas to leave town as soon as possible. But before they left, Paul and Silas visited their friends in town again and told them more stories about Jesus.

ALEX'S STORY

My name is Alex. I live by the sea and we get a lot of storms here in the winter, strong winds – even hurricanes. That's bad for the sailors, but good for my family because our job is to mend sails ripped by the ferocious winds. But some ships are too badly damaged to be mended.

Many ships get wrecked on the rocks near our island. Often a bit of sail gets washed ashore and we carry it home, to be used for patches on larger sails.

Sometimes when a ship is wrecked, everyone is drowned. My father remembers a hurricane that wrecked a ship just off the island, but all two hundred and seventy-six people reached shore safely. Now that has to be a miracle! They say it was because God promised Paul, who was one of the passengers, that he would save them.

49
Shipwreck!

Paul travelled the world, telling people about Jesus. He often faced danger, as the Jewish leaders particularly wanted to kill him. He spent many years in prison, but used this time well, telling prisoners, jailers and soldiers how Jesus died and came to life again. Because Paul was a Roman citizen, he had a right to be judged in Rome, so he travelled there by ship.

It was the season of stormy winds in the Mediterranean and the ship kept being blown off course. Paul warned the ship's captain that it was too risky to continue the journey, but he wouldn't listen. A hurricane blew up near the Greek island of Crete and everyone was sure they would drown.

'Why didn't you listen to me?' said Paul. 'We are sure to be shipwrecked

now, but God has promised me that none of us will die!'

They endured many days of violent storms, then they hit shallow waters. The sailors wanted to try to get ashore in a small boat, but again Paul warned them against it.

'Let's stay and build up our strength by having a meal,' he said. 'God will save us!'

At last they spied land, but the ship hit a sandbank and broke up. There were soldiers on board, who were taking the prisoners back to Rome. They wanted to kill them all to stop them escaping. But Julius, a Roman centurion, stopped them because he wanted to save Paul. Everyone was able to swim to shore or hang on to broken bits of the ship until they were rescued.

The island they landed on was called Malta. There Paul survived the bite of a deadly snake with no ill effects and also healed the governor of the island, who was very ill. He stayed there all through the season of winter storms, preaching the good news of Jesus Christ to everyone he met.

MARY'S STORY

I am Mary and I live in Carmel. My sisters and I often wonder what it will be like in heaven. My father is a great scholar and has studied all the Scriptures. He knows a story told by the great disciple John, who was a good friend of Jesus. It's about a vision of heaven that John saw while he was praying.

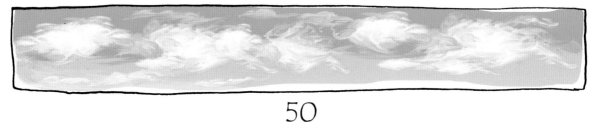

50
A New Heaven and a New Earth

'I saw the new heaven and new earth that God will make for us in the future. It had a holy city like Jerusalem, only much more beautiful, like a bride wearing the finest clothes for her new husband. The city has walls made of twelve different layers of precious jewels, gates of pearl and the streets are made of pure transparent gold, like glass.

'The crystal river of life, which flows from the throne of God, runs through the centre of the city. It is there for everyone to drink. On each side of the splendid river are trees of life, bearing a fresh crop of fruit each month.

'There is no need for the sun and the moon any more, because the glory of God is so bright it lights up everywhere. Inside the beautiful city are all the people who have asked God to forgive them and whose names are now written in the book of life.

'When the new heaven and earth come, the past and every sort of evil will be gone and we will live with God for ever. We will never be unhappy again because God will wipe away every tear from our eyes. There will be no more crying or pain or death and peace and love will remain in his new world for ever.'

105